NOIR

[OR, WHEN THE NIGHT COMES]

DEREK R. KING

Noir
[Or, When the Night Comes]

2nd Edition © 2025 by Derek R. King

Second Edition ISBN 978-1-965455-01-2
eBook available

First edition 2020
ISBN: 978-0-9992523-4-5

All rights reserved. No part of this publication may be reproduced, stored or transmitted in any form or by any means, electronic, mechanical, photocopying, recording, scanning, or otherwise without written permission from the publisher. It is illegal to copy this book, post it to a website, or distribute it by any other means without permission.

Derek R. King asserts the moral right to be identified as the author of this work.

Derek R. King has no responsibility for the persistence or accuracy of URLs for external or third-party Internet Websites referred to in this publication and does not guarantee that any content on such Websites is, or will remain, accurate or appropriate.

Because of the dynamic nature of the Internet, any web addresses or links contained in this book may have changed since publication and may no longer be valid. e views expressed in this work are solely those of the author and do not necessarily reflect the views of the publisher, and the publisher hereby disclaims any responsibility for them.

Image Credits
Cover Art: "Birch Woods, Moonlight," mixed media by Jane Cornwell. https://www.janecornwell.co.uk

Any people depicted in stock imagery provided by Pixabay Images are models, and such images are being used for illustrative purposes only.

Image I (Noir), Image by zhugher from Pixabay https://pixabay.com/photos/mysterious- fog-path-forest-5323020/ Pixabay License: Free for commercial use. No attribution required.

Image II (Gothic), Image by Syaibatul Hamdi from Pixabay https://pixabay.com/photos/wanderer-mysterious-mystic-mystical-5297457/ Pixabay License: Free for commercial use. No attribution required.

Image III (Mean Streets), Image by Public Domain Images from Pixabay https://bit.ly/2FJQGPE Pixabay License: Free for commercial use. No attribution required.
Image IV (Embrace), Image by croisy from Pixabay https://pixabay.com/photos/slim-girl-beautiful-model-1391235/ Pixabay License: Free for commercial use. No attribution required.

To and for my Muse, as always and forevermore

Acknowledgement

The author warmly thanks Sarah at 8N Publications for bringing the first edition of this work into the world in 2020 (ISBN 978-0-999252-34-5). As my first poetry collection, it remains especially dear to me—opening the door for so many wonderful things that followed.

My deepest gratitude to my lovely wife, Julie Kusma, whose encouragement and faith in these words inspired me to return to them, and to share them anew in this second edition.

Contents

I

Welcome 2
Tempest 3
Pendulum 4
The Healing Despair 5
Shhh 6
Blissful arrest 7
Strange Days 8
Divine Grotesque 10
Phantom 11
ego eram 12
Unfold 13
Vanquished 14
Armchair Wrestling 16
acquiescence 17
Alone 18
Invocation 19
Silent Riposte 21
Pigeon 22
Endless 23
Shadowlands 24
Epitaph 25
Creation's darkness 26
Into The Black 27

II
Path less Travelled.................................... 30
Hypnotist 33
Vampyre 34
The Haunting 35
Violin Concerto...................................... 36
Poison 37
Chasing Skies 38
The Night Shades 39
Crows 40
The Attic.. 41
Redemption.. 42
Dark, Heart, Ways (The Recital)....................... 44
Frosted Talons....................................... 46
Sacred sacraments 47
Lost.. 49
Kraken... 50
Abbott Black... 51
Perpetual Endings.................................... 52
Verité... 53
Silent Mirror.. 54
White Chipped Cup 55
The Exquisite Devine 56
Blessed Be 57
My Evangeline 58
Tethered 59

III
The Unseen (or Beyond the Veil)....................... 62
No Place Like Home................................... 63
Heroes... 64
Glass Eyes 65

The Actor. 66
Fix 68
Vesting. 69
Beached. 70
Treadmill of Despair
(A Butterfly Caught) 72
Desolation Alley 74
Subway Rats 75
Strychnine Kids. 76
Snowblind 77
Streets 78
Lazarus 79
Because We're Young. 80
Trapped in Ecstasy 81
Stranger Danger 82
Intricate 83
Classifieds 84
Hope Eraser 85

IV
The Endless Beginnings 88
Enchanting 89
Crimson. 90
Evermore. 91
Amore 92
Red Rose 93
Deserts 94
Prayer 95
Medusa 96
Blissful Cataclysm 97
Carousel. 98
Breathe 99
Cat O' Nine Tails 101

Crush	102
Frenzy	103
Killing Zone	104
Black is the ardour	105
Departure	106
Setting Sun	107
Embrace	108
Delicate	110
Sleeping Muse	111
Siren	112
Celestial	113
Moonlit Shadowed Seas	114
Enchanted	115
Euphoria	116
Pearls	117
La Volta	118
Serene Surrender	119
Index of Poems with First Lines	121
About the Author	125
About the Cover Designer	126
Also by Derek R. King	127

I

Welcome

You want dark?
I can oblige.
I am the dark.
The blackness,
the dream stealer,
the truth,
the reality.
Speak or spare,
you decide.
A limited choice,
a limited time.

You decide, but
before the hour
when night-time falls,
and lights go out for
passions abound.
Choose your masque,
for it is your time.
You begin,
to see
All that you
have
become.

Tempest

I am born of
Fire and Tempest.
The Eternal conflict
to feed the Flame.
Drawn of Darkness
ever needing,
Gnarled and Wretched
In silent scream.
Love and Rage
unwed companions,
Entwined forever in
bitter Embrace.
Fighting for my
Soul's survival.
Day and Night
They claim the Game.

Pendulum

I have heard of this
(Happiness)
of which you speak.
Seems it's not for me
or my creed.
For at the precipice
of light and dark,
we fight this thing
with all our hearts.
Pendulum swings
to and fro,
nowhere to hide
nowhere to go.
At the edge,
we must do battle
with hearts and minds
or else
unravel.

The Healing Despair

Feel the poison
in the mist
sense its pain,
feel it twist.
Hidden below thought
and prayer,
hangs the poison
in its layer.

Biting sudden
grasping hand,
sense the panic
driving mad.
Holding silent
in the air
departs the poison,
leaving despair.

Shhh

If it's dark
it must be night.
But night still
Cold, air linger,
Chill, quiet,
soft yet harsh.
Distant senses
heed the call.
A single, solitary
water drop falls
crashing like a cymbal
in the still of night
in the darkness
a blinding light.

Blissful arrest

I feel a cold wind
upon my back.
I feel its icy fingers
pass through my flesh,
wrapping slowly around
my lung and
softly,
place its steely fingers
within me
in loose grip.
It is a gentle caress
of frigid air.
Subdued,
lulling to deep
surrender,
slumber
and darkness.

Strange Days

The cavalcade of freaks
and the side street show,
run down the city streets.
The jamboree band
cacophony
is calling to you
and me.

Strange days,
strange ways,
induced by my
only nightmare.

There's flesh for sale
but she's looking pale.
"Spend some time,
come with me."
She's as long as she's tall,
walking down the hall
but I cannot see her shadow.

Strange days,
strange ways,
induced by my
only nightmare.

In the house of freaks,
you will always meet,
face to face
your own reflection.
But do not despair
for there is no one there,
only fools dare
to question.

Strange days,
strange ways,
induced by my
only nightmare.

Divine Grotesque

Turn away,
Now!
Feed your eyes no more.
I feel a wraith,
wretched,
tortured,
twisted,
gnarled.

My whitening,
hollowing,
translucent flesh,
concealed from you,
but not all.

A cadaver with a pulse,
like Halloween on a bad day.
My sunken eyes
in blackened sockets
see you,
holding you in trance-like stare.
All that I have become
I can only feel,
but your eyes,
your face,
are like a
mirror to me.
YOU are the horror
Turn away now. Please?

Phantom

What say you to this?
That I become in my pain.
That light passes through me,
In daytime,
such that I am gone,
transparent to all
and into beyond.
At night I become one
with darkness.
Whose cold caress
embraces me and lifts me.
It folds me and holds me,
caressing and soothing,
I become its one.
Suspended, timeless,
enveloped in motionless,
blackness.
Its darkest hour,
a spiral haze, where
confusion removed,
pain removed,
sorrow removed,
and then,
the light.

ego eram

Something stirring in the gutter,
come take my hand and set me free.
Come feel and see the power and glory,
come see my kingdom conquer me.

I am.

Visualise my monster creation,
I beg you please to heed my plea.
But I am standing alone and waiting,
as my monster becomes me.

I was.

Unfold

Making monsters
in the corridors of our minds.
Scary monsters
cowering from the blind.
Meet me in the garden
where the sun shines
in the night,
by the moon tower's
shallowing light.
In the maelstrom,
a poison called love eats at the heart
withering its love.

Vanquished

Hold fast you monsters!
My time is not yet come.
I see you,
I see you.

Flying night time
coming pain.
Pain, it's my pleasure
to beat you.
To kill to… not me,
to be alone
for all time.

Time is here you monsters!
Kill the switch,
kill the cure.
Feast on me,
take your fill.
You are a poison
doomed to die.
Linger if you must,
host my body
if you will.

My spirit is mine,
it transcends you,
it sees you.
Sees you and
seizes you,
TIGHT.
It dwarfs you,
smothers you,
you see, you see,
for now you are me.

Armchair Wrestling

Sitting in my armchair,
think I'm going
insane.
Panes of glass are
broken,
clouds float by
again.
Painted frames,
flaked and dry
rain streams in
from stormy skies.
The muslin net that
you once loved
now covers you
upon our bed.
Every day's a
nightmare,
because you're
no longer here
but the bottle
by my left
dulls this pain.

acquiescence

Drawing blood and
prickling pain,
trickling blood
like snow in rain.

Truth is torture,
points thrust home,
ripping flesh and
piercing bone.

Mistakes of life
nostalgic lament
weeping wounds,
a blood rent.

Numb with guilt,
an anguished cry,
leaves shivering lips
and panicking eyes.

A bed of nails,
my deathbed is.
Searing pain.
No bed of Roses.

Alone

I walk the path
alone
in sorrow.
I walk the path
alone
in pain.
I feel the sun is
setting,
shadows calling me,
once again.

Invocation

Sometimes,
when I'm all alone
I feel the demons
rising in my mind.
Operation doctor
seems to me just
like an infinite
waste of time.

Shards of my memory
fleet in and out like shadows
in the passageways
of my tortured mind.
I dream in colour every night,
my waking day
I live in black
and white.

Can you hear the words
of the psycho seer?
Preaching delirium
from his psycho-sphere.

Within all confusion random images
filter through my mind.
Savage and relentless
destroying any peace that I might find.
Delirious with passion like a spating river
in full flow.
Tormented and demented
I don't bleed blood,
I bleed much more.
I bleed my soul.

Silent Riposte

Say no more,
I've heard it all before.
Deaf words fall
on dumb stones.
I hear your words
don't say anymore.

I can hear
your sound
that's spoken in my ear
I can hear your noises,
your noises
are too clear.

Your words are spoken
but hold no truth.
No feelings of love
or passion.
I feel what you say
that you don't mean.
Say no more.

Don't blind me,
with your words of cruel.
In deafening silence
I store the truth
I store the TRUTH.
Say no more.

Stunned into silence
your words are insincere
stunned into silence
hollow words in silence die.
Stunned into silence
no capitulation.

Pigeon

Drowning is proportional
to suicide in pairs.
Additional complexities
make patients very rare.
Analysed and categorised
and filed in darkened drawers.
Deemed to be too difficult,
so just another lost cause.

Endless

It is the time of darkness,
a time of pain.
Left lying on a shelf,
dust covered, not vain.
Allowed to wallow as
challengers rise in cold grip.
Portolan denied.
In hungry warrant
with blood shot eyes
drink drunk on
remorse a plenty.
Philosophers lies,
bright and shining
in dapple hues
turn swift the light
that I might with
crystal fuse.

Shadowlands

Walking through
Shadowlands, I'm
walking all alone.
Nothing left here,
and
chilled to the bone.
Feel the mists encircling
caressing scars of pain.
Like pure sea salt
in open wounds,
I will heal again.

But there is a
darkness growing,
devouring my soul.
I call your name
across the void,
silence only
in reply.
Pure and cold and
empty here,
so I think of you.
Will you guide me
safely
home?

Epitaph

These are not just words
that fill this space
they are my soul.
On a page with graphite
laid out and bare,
for those who care to
need to see.
Sometimes light,
sometimes not,
But always and forever
True.
An epitaph for me.

Creation's darkness

Stars of darkness
fill the night,
burning fusion,
twisted flyht.
Creation's darkness
folds with grace,
treatise of heat,
convolving space
crucible of lightning
stimuli of light
energy crushing
Dark
Black
Night.

Into The Black

On a distant planet,
at the furthest shore,
across the Black Sea,
I watch for you.

Dark clouds fill the sky,
the air is still,
across the Wasteland,
the River spills.

I walk across the Barren Plain,
devoid of love
and wracked with pain,
Longing for the healing Rain.
Into the Black.
In to the
Black.

II

Path less Travelled

The path which brought me here
was long and meandering,
a hillside path.
The last section
rolled down and out before me
towards my destination.
I could just make out the river,
glistening in the moonlight.
Gentle ripples,
caught momentarily
in the silvery glow,
mesmerizing,
flowing on their way.

I don't really know
if it's day or night here.
The clocks changed recently,
you see.
So it is very difficult to tell,
except that it is dark,
save for the moonlight.

Nearing the river,
I see a wooden boat.
Long, thin tapering,
like a gondola
a seat across the centre.
As I approach
I see it is weary with age,
softly worn by the passage of time,
exposing smoothed grains.
It's a very shallow boat,
clearly built to glide.

A drifting cloud dims the brightness.

"This river runs dry sometimes,"
the voice said,
"we have to be careful of the shallows."
I turn to face the "voice"
but it is already behind me,
outlined in silhouette
by the once more,
bright moonlight.

For the first time I notice
how very wide the river is.
No longer the narrow
silvery ribbon braid from afar,
but a wide shimmering,
powerful ribbon.

The boat creaks gently, its moorings
rise and fall with the soft ebb and flow,
soothing, caressing waters lap against
its worn timbers.

There is a great peacefulness
about this place,
with these gentle sounds,
I am at ease.
A deep breath of contentment
leaves my body.
"Welcome to the River Styx,"
the voice says.

Hypnotist

Haunting memories
of the hypnotist,
a man in black,
the sidewalk twist.

A golden timepiece
tick tocks the time,
as sands in the hourglass
rise slowly upwards from
below,
while candles burn
that have no glow.

A bender of minds,
a Master of Distraction
or simply just
the action's reaction.

Vampyre

Love me.
Feed on me.
I will be,
your vampyre.

The Haunting

It haunts me sometimes
in silhouette form.
Disorientated features
from me it hides.
Large curling horns,
radiate from
triangular head.
Tall, caped in black
standing, waiting,
in perfect silence
no gesture made.
It defies existence.
Waiting,
it haunts me.

Violin Concerto

The violin concerto
screams loudly in my head
turning my world
a bright fiery red.
Its sound torments me,
the illusions distress me,
its time annoys me,
their days are come.
But none to end
forever demented
and trapped within
their shrieking tones,
in this unholy cacophony.

Poison

In a hollow empty room,
filled with darkness,
filled with gloom.
Hear the poison in the air,
soft and silent
seeping from its lair.
But driven by
deep despair,
upon wings of darkness,
their hopes and prayers,
they placed their
faith.

Chasing Skies

Rendered fire and lightning
chase the sky
across the horizon,
until time's end.
The end of time.
When darkness folds the Earth
back into Mother Space.
Peace,
peace
at last.

The Night Shades

Nothing's sacred
outside the ivory tower.
Into the blackness
the nightshade grows.
A realm where
silhouettes gather
and mirrors pose
and poison pens,
in tortured hands,
stab broken minds
to drive them mad.

While sweet derisions
patronise
like a kiss from them
and their lying eyes.
Here on after
looking glass
across fields of flowers
and woodland grass.
Beyond pale rivers
and sallow seas
where poppies grown
and cast their seeds
Barron Waste.

Crows

"I was born before the crows,
they gathered,
from all around they came,
high they soared
to witness and watch
my birth
and scatter the ashes."

*"We sit in trees
with feathers black
and greying beak.
We sit and watch
the human reek,
like carrion fowl, (we are)."
And when you're done
Your life blood spilled
take flight we shall
once more for thee."*

The Attic

Wind blows through
broken attic windows,
shrieking like some little girl.
All my toys
are in the attic,
they are all
my only friends.

Redemption

"How may I help you my Son,
what do you seek?"

"Redemption."

"Come into the light
so I might see you better.
You look unwell!"

*"I am the undead,
last of my kind
persecuted by you monks.
I shall hunt down and…..
in the name of your lord."*

"You are confused,
the fever makes you
say these things, my son.
Come inside,
come inside now."

*"In the name of your Lord
you took my child,
you killed my wife,
you left me to rot
in iron cage hung
from the old Tallow tree.
You thought me dead but,
the creature set me free....."*

"You, you're…….."

*"…..and now I have come for thee,
Repent."*

Dark, Heart, Ways (The Recital)

This cross I bear.
the need justified the end,
the end justifies the means,
the means justifies the need.
This cross I bear.

Dark is the tunnel
cold are the eyes,
a hint of misplaced trust,
no sign of loving.
The tunnel is dark.

Dark is the tunnel
and the serpentine tongue,
licks the wounds of passion,
no sign of kindness.
The tunnel is dark.

Dark is the tunnel,
bloodless as the heart,
that torments the tortured body,
no sign of giving.
The tunnel is dark.

Dark is the tunnel,
barbed as the hand,

a hand that shook in friendship,
no sign of feeling.
The tunnel is dark.

Dark is the tunnel,
like the love of their ways,
a dark bottomless chasm,
no sign of being.
The tunnel is dark.
This cross I bear.

Frosted Talons

Still,
dark and still.
Frosted talons in the night
scratch the panes
'til rays of light,
shine through and hold
the mist.
Dank
and heavy,
hanging, lingering.
Through the pain,
and to the chest
grips the lungs
squeezing
breath
from far beyond,
the glacial seas.

Sacred sacraments

Sacred sallow
Hallowed hours
Teasing twilight
Moaning moon
Silver sky
Groaning ground.
Twisted timbers
Barren branches
Gnarled knots.
Chaotic chorus
Triumphant tune.
Slowly screeching
Distant dawning
Clawing closer
Ju Ju Ju Ju jamboree.
Sleeping silent
Pleasant people
Rest resplendent.
Clacking clocks
Tolls tormenting
Precedes parade.
Figures foul
Silhouetted scars
Haunt horizon's
Moonlit mews.
Bitter broken
Tortured twisted
Cacophony crescendo
Dance divine

Waltzing walkers
Silent streets
Anarchic angels,
Majestic manifest.

Lost

Where once was love,
now there's none.
T'was not the key
she placed on
my tongue,
but a draft of
Belladonna.

Kraken

The Kraken rises, high
from waters dark
and deep,
cursing loudly
in the air.
Always loudly,
never playful
slashing claws cut
through the air
and wave.
Piercing eyes rip through
sea green glare,
horned devil head
horizon scouring
seeking out
the next true full storm.

Abbott Black

A little rhyme
a winter chill,
too dark this night
for monastic thrills.
To seek by chance,
a friendly ghost?
Not a chance
this night's
Unholy host.
For Abbott Black
here did dwell,
who sent the townsfolk
Straight to Hell....

Inside this place,
lived Abbott Black,
renowned poisoner,
from centuries back.
Draw in close,
you still can hear
clank of crock
and pot,
as he mixes up
his next batch,
of lethal drops.

Perpetual Endings

It is a dark night
when the haunting comes.
A chastened and bitten
fevered
night time sojourn.
Uncontrolled sensation
grip in an instant.
fevered shaking,
loosing,
drifting,
demanding,
taken,
smothered,
eases grip,
slow release,
means no harm.
Gripping controlling
Fevered,
Shrinking,
Demanding,
Loosing,
Drifting,
Taken,
snatched
until the end.

Verité

Torment the dance in opiate haze
pale drawn and lilac
the skins soft malaise.
In red bright and dazzling
and copper's fiery burn
let loose the voices, scream
in silent hum.
Oh, the drone of silence
is too much to bear
let loose in anger
madness and despair.

Silent Mirror

Green light shines in sodium haze,
recalls memoirs of opium days.
Ostrich feathers in the hall,
tapestries hanging on marble walls.

Up the stairway hidden steep,
a tall black figure silently weeps.
Knowing all but all unknown,
tales beyond this twilight zone.

Unholy silence fills the air,
across the hall below the stair.
A garland falls in ghostly white,
Casting shadows in the night.

Draped up on the paneled walls,
Painted portraits scream in demented call.
Beyond all hope the silent mirrors,
rationalise their ghostly shimmer.

Caught up in a dream divine,
where fantasy and blood entwine.
Upon the stairway the figure calls,
unto the garland in the hall.

White Chipped Cup

In this cup of coffee
the poison floats.
A poison
so deep,
black and
endless,
just like you
a poison too.

In the broken mirror
broken faces stare.
In this
coffee cup
a woken poison's there.
Black and endless,
just like you
a poison.

But in the nighttime
Darkness,
there is no poison.
No poison there
only pain.
But just like you
the pain seeps
through.

The Exquisite Devine

Hark,
I hear an angel in
the wings.
A gentle breath brushes
against my cheek,
its soothing caress
comforts me.
In my darkest days, and
brightest nights,
my comfort
my succour,
to give me peace,
to give me rest.

I beseech you,
tarry a while,
linger longer.
I yearn for
your comfort,
'tis unkind we cannot
embrace.
To be enveloped in
your kindly
grace
fills me with such joy,
I cannot put into words.
Yet time may heal this
barrier between us,
that I may at some time be.

Blessed Be

It is my craving.
It is my need,
my muse.
To bring me here, to
this dark valley of
blackness silver lights
and deepest reds.

A wilderness of
Passion's pain
where death lies,
and waits for me.
My release,
embrace me,
release me,
my pleasure
is yours.

My Evangeline

We touch
and the darkness
recoils
to its lair.
A loathsome,
hungry, snarling
beast.

For we are
Divine,
lost souls are we,
too careless
to live
but forever
to be.
My Evangeline.

Tethered

Claustrophobic.
That's how my brain
feels in my skull.
Tethered,
screaming
crying,
to break free.
Escape
the drudgery of life
unfulfilled
suppressed
emotions.

To fulfill
wildest
passions
dreams.
To sip from the
Cup of Dionysus,
until
drink no more
and feed my soul
to poetry's
muse.

III

The Unseen
(or Beyond the Veil)

Walk with me
through fields of glass,
a nightmare dance
that will never last.

Fools imagine
the lights stand still,
who among you
will take this pill?

Hear them calling
from streets of pain,
the lost and the wretched
who bleed with shame.

No Place Like Home

I love this place,
the smell of dying rust.
I love this place,
when the casino goes bust.
I love this place,
the streets that bleed.
I love this place,
corrosions offspring seed.
I love this place,
spewing out decay.
I love this place,
where the priests always prey.
I love this place,
when it screams out the lights.
I love this place,
how it beckons me in the night.

Heroes

Emaciated heroes
crave the limelight of the street.
Leather desperadoes
feed the panic and the beat.

Nights are dark and cold as ice,
the wind slices to the bone.
Only fools and those who breed there
come to this forbidden zone.

Graffiti walls a cornerstone
where territories end.
For those who dare to trespass,
forever meet their end.

Glass Eyes

Walking down
the side street show
hear footsteps
that start to grow
turn around
there's no-thing there.
Darkness blinds
with cunning lust
where's your faith?
Where's your trust?
Panic, abandon,
screaming with fear
savage, relentless,
draws forth a tear.
Nothing left to
feel or do
when night-time nothings
give chase to you.

The Actor

Black out sights
from red lights grow
hints the face
behind the show.
They died a death,
still born breath.

Stage is set
for worthless actors
sold before costs
by the talentless factor.
They died a death
still born breath.

Gas light burns
above left stage door
tears run down
on clown's so low.
They died a death
still born breath.

Faerie lights
on cuddly toys.
Pink for girls,
blue for boys.
Street lights shine
betray the joys.
Pimps for girls,
knives for boys.
They died a death
still born breath.

Fix

"How much for me?"
the girl cried.
"How much, how much?"
Clothes hang limp
from wretched shoulders
emaciated, bedraggled
unkempt, but clean.
"How much for me"
"how much for me, mister?"

No takers tonight.
In silent gaze
obscured by revulsion
passing by, passing by.
"How much for me mister?"
The cry repeats
and fades
into the night
A simple fix.

Vesting

Pressure!
Vice like
pressure
grips my
brain.
Pain.
The fear of
failure,
letting you down,
constant victories
and success,
breeds a
disappointment,
Unlike the rest.

Beached

Sleazy DayGlo of birds
on the wing,
aroma of cheap perfume and
the hot flesh of sin.

Below the neon
they do entice
take hold of clients
in this sweat-stained
paradise.

Spandex shorts get tighter when
there's a needle to feed
"Screw me hard and
fill my need."

Washed up and washed out
on a beach of satin sheets.
The needle sparkles softly
and then it retreats.
Release the body but
screw the brain.
Satiated,
release the pain.

In the alley,
the trash can grave
a home for those who
seem depraved
in this twilight zone
a mystic lure for
those who crave
their autocratic vices.

Treadmill of Despair
(A Butterfly Caught)

Sirens scream
teenage SOS
torn up on the highways
as fantasy pricks the brain.

She likes telling sensual stories
she sells fantasies from behind the screen.
She cries treading water drowning
in her nightmare slowly dying.

She knows where her so called art lies
she eats up all the eyes that drool.
She reads over all the news so slowly
makes the headlines seldom but only.

She's living a lie, not a legend
she cries all alone, in her room.
She waits in the wings like a phantom
some things just aren't what they seem.
(All she really wants is a dream.)

She tastes the fruit of lesson five
she fakes the nerve with uncanny smile.
She cries out loud but it's in vain
she doesn't sense the pleasure's pain.

Sirens scream
teenage SOS
torn up on the highways
discarded in the rain.

Desolation Alley

Desolation Alley
where the rats come out to play.
Desolation Alley
where the only hope's beyond the grave.
(We bid you welcome).

"Back on the streets ain't got no ties
I'm sick of lookin' at your lyin' eyes.
Your sweet talk words mean nothing to me
so climb down here, come bitch with me.

Standing here like trashcans of flesh
everyone's screamin' I'm the fucking best.
We don't give a shit we all let go
got ripped up jeans and a barbed wire halo.

You can screw your coke, your heroin, your hash
but gimme some booze 'cause I wanna get smashed.
Law and order are on the run, cause we are back
And we're number 1."

Subway Rats

Lying in the subway
with a switchblade in his back,
cured of subway madness
by the flick and then the crack.

Colour wasted bloody walls
scream loudly in the night,
swearing bloody vengeance
in the dank stiletto light.

Subway rats move in to kill,
no shelter any more
subway rats are beckoning
in the Metro's silent roar.

Strychnine Kids

Stalking the alleys like a Punch and Judy show,
looks like death as the funeral grows.
Ever slowly maddening as pain and fever glow,
twisting at the bit,
Strychnine kids.

Fools obey when the door's locked tight,
accept the invite to this strange delight.
A burning styles us as illusions fade and grow,
bleeding from the lips
Strychnine kids.

Strychnine kids
screaming with the pain,
clawing at their brain,
writhing in the gutter,
tearing at their veins,
spewing bloody rain,
their dealer's on their lips,
Strychnine kids.

Snowblind

See them all
catch a fire.
Snow blind upon
the pyre.
Watching them
a snitch in time
saves.
Burning,
comes and goes.
Talking in foreign tongues
shrinking in,
foreign minds.
Dying in reality
they are,
"Be saved"
The mirror crack
white wire dreams
forever confident
is not what it
seems.

Streets

Streets that run with anger
Streets that run with hate
Streets that run with blood
Streets are in full spate.

Minds are filled with deception
Minds are filled with lies
Minds are filled with vengeance
Vivid in the mind's eye.

Humans torn and mangled
Humans battle pained
Humans thrive off possessions
Let those humans play those games.

Lazarus

Wispy shadows walk
the boardwalk at night.
Tortured bodies crave
sanctuary from the light.
Gnarled fingers scrape
and scratch flaking flesh.
Torn mouths take in
their last breath.

Decaying take pennies
from eyes of the dead.
The lost seek revenge
tearing their flesh from
their heads.
Their wailing cries
pierce and take flight.
Rise up Lazarus, for this
is your time tonight.

Because We're Young

Because we're young
we live and breathe
we walk on water
we are invincible.

Because we're young
we drink and eat
we love and fight
we need no sleep.

Because we're young
we see through your lies
we rise and yell
we untether from your hell.

Because we're young
We empathise
Because
We
Are
Young.

Trapped in Ecstasy

Martyred by your fashioned love
put your hand into my heart.
Warped by your sublime devotion
I'm twisted by your derision emotions.
Yet here I am rejoicing
when I'm captivated in your arms
entangled in the distant mesh
of your seldom pleasant charms.

Stranger Danger

We talk of spies
with shadowed eyes,
in long raincoats
and steaming rain
seeking refuge
in sheltered doorways.

Silenced gunshots
cold steel and lead.
Wax-like melting body
slides gently down
rough brick wall
a graceful descent to
wet cobblestones,
rest for
evermore.

Intricate

A Spider's Web of deceit
and lies.
Who to trust
to live or die.
Weaves a tale,
of complex lives.
The intricate footsteps
tiptoe of spies.
Who've won and lost,
and risen once more.
To play the game,
and even the score.

Classifieds

"Blood shot eyes,
mourn lost decaying buildings,
childhood memoirs,
of a man who is the same."

"Unshaven face,
seeks love and understanding,
but never ever realised
that it was always there."

"Dressed down body,
craves last and final resting place,
a final plea for mercy,
to a land that doesn't care."

Hope Eraser

A haze of light in the alley grows,
the hate in the night of the child shows,
upon the wall the spray can reads
like a faerie tale of disbelief.

Burning and charring the carrion waste,
no time for living, haste, haste, haste
Yet in the night the quarantine grows,
like a vetting game at fairground shows.

While on the water jetsam floats,
in the skyrise the pinstripe gloats.
Upon the wall the writing is clear,
in the night best hide your fears.

IV

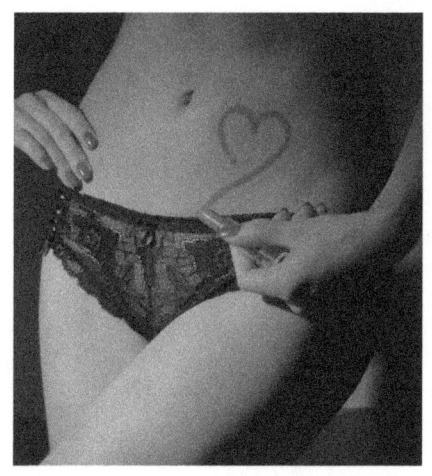

The Endless Beginnings

Open up the door and come inside
turn the lock, turn the day into night.
Welcome to this strange delight,
Turn out the lights.

Draw in close and have no fear,
there is no pain, only pleasure here.
A cornucopia of ecstasy
when you are next to me.

Enchanting

Hidden in the darkness
by faintest candlelight
I picture you
a vision of heaven.
Innocence of beauty
shimmering in white,
like snow,
in moonlight.
Sweetest love ever known
lingers in the hollows.
She is, glowing
with love
flickering,
enchanting
in the night.

Crimson

Red is the colour of my passion dream
a deep crimson, full bodied
pulsating, sensuous, pulsating
in veins, the deep throbbing veins.

Dark is the colour of the night
deepest blue from the depths
of oceans.
A cloak of lightness
to engulf the soul
as time passes time.

White silver is the colour of the light
that draws me near
to sweet escape
an ecstasy of pure and true
to cleanse my thought
and purge my soul.

Evermore

Hold the dream
like a heart on fire
climb the mountains of desire
succumb to the pleasures
of passion's fire
and share the gift.
Entwined together
let love grow
higher
enveloped by
emotions
in love
evermore.

Amore

Between the sheets
behind closed curtains,
dwells the realm of feel to see.
Wandering fingertips like
meandering glances,
caress the body
of those who need.

Shining eyes meet
in the darkness.
Eyes we close in
innocence bliss.
Soft moans of pleasure
leave ruby lips.
A gentle touch,
A secret kiss.
A silent whisper,
the souls release.

Red Rose

How sweet the perfume graces me
from love's full scented rose.
It's ruby petals soft
like my lady's skin
glistening and sparkling
in the night time airs.
Moonlit and serene
she glides to me.

Deserts

A cloak of darkness
hides the tears,
of long lost love
and summer fears.
Hidden far
across the night
to dance in faintest
candle light.
Holding close
the flickering grows,
scent as sight
for those who chose,
to rest a while
in darkness sweet,
and feel soft sands
upon their feet.
And rest a while
in deep embrace
unburdened by love
in this gentle place.

Prayer

"He lies in bed never looking at me,
he lies in bed never holding or touching me
he lies in bed not talking to me
he lies in bed, think he's ignoring me.

There's something wrong in my lover's mind
they're grinding him down
turning him blind
to me.

And I feel rejected and insecure
like I'm standing on a rock in the middle of
a sea of emotion
distressed devotion takes
its hold on me.

Confused by thoughts of hidden fears
my eyes in pain bleed stinging tears
my body shakes, I want him near
oh I really need to have him here,
with me."

Medusa

In the world of darkness
the clouds don't dance.
Where the moon is black
and darkened, a haunting
waits for me there.

There are no eyes of kindness
no loving words to hear.
The only sounds from those red lips
whisper bloody thoughts
and fear.

Trophies in the passageway
fate at its wits end.
A dressed in black, femme fatale
with rose red lips
sells passion to all
who dare.

Blissful Cataclysm

What pain is this
that taunts me now?
Torments my soul
in deepest depth
where darkest passion's
longings hide.
Deep desires linger,
intense to touch,
to taste
can sense them,
the longing hurts
and gnaws
and twists,
convulsions in agony
and ecstasy,
give me release.
I cannot breathe
by deep desire
smothered
sweeps over me.
Wave upon wave rages
through my body.
Over flesh, haunting,
taunting,
from deepest secrets
no escape.

Carousel

She moves just like
a carousel
casting wicked
wanton spells.
Selling dreams
and fantasies
swimming soft in
satin seas.
And through the night
in dark embrace
I see her glowing
smiling face.
An alluring mystery
but oh so sweet.

Breathe

"Breathe in,
breathe in
the dark,
breathe in,
breathe in
the black.
Breathe in,
breathe in for me,
Breathing,
out and in."

The stars are out
the sky is dark,
weaving
mysterious art.
And through a mist
of primeval sin,
a Voodoo dolly
in a little black dress says,

"Breathe in,
breathe in
the dark,
breathe in,
breathe in
the black.
Breathe in,
breathe in for me,
Breathing,
out and in,
breathe in,
breathe in for me,
my darlin'"

Cat O' Nine Tails

Lipstick words
upon the mirror,
hanging on
the bathroom wall.
"Lots of love,
hate to leave you
loved to tease you,
cat o' nine tails."

Heavy scent in
the boudoir lingers,
a tousled bed that
knows no shame.
Please to lead and
pleased to follow,
touch the hollows
cat o' nine tails.

Black and white and
red carnations,
mark the place where
pleasures end.
Touch my life
and heal to suffer
feel my sadness,
cat o' nine tails.

Crush

Belts and buckles
and shackles and chains
whips and leather
and screams of pain.
Rubber and latex and
fishnets and 'hose
toys and ticklers
and a wink that knows.

Satins and lace and
feathers and fur,
stilettos or barefoot
and a pussycat purr.
Lipstick and rouge
and mascara and ice
eyeshadow and
polish.
Oooh, this
is nice.

Frenzy

A feeding frenzy
in passion's embrace
no time to lose.
Lips entwine like
melding wax
held, but no move. Then
frantic heads turn
to and fro,
too little time
too much
to lose.
Want it all
want it now
fall upon the
silken beach.
Outstretched
sinews straining
until the last
breaths and
clutches are
released.

Killing Zone

In the killing zone
of love's embrace,
surrender to the pleasures of
passion's grace.
The silken touch,
serene and soothing.
Love entwined,
slowly moving.

Dissolved of all will in
this pleasure affliction.
Feed the passion,
ease the addiction.
The scent of love is
passion's fuel.
Taste the scent,
kiss the jewel.

Sense the passion,
feel the pain.
Held together in
sweet embrace.
Entwined together,
entwined together.

Succumb to the pleasures
of love's addiction.
Succumb to the thrill
of the ultimate sedation.

Black is the ardour

Black is the ardour
cold as ice,
tinged with hatred,
malice and vice.
Take a chair,
there's one for you there,
cloak you in darkness,
sorrow and despair.
No puerile pleasures,
here await,
a cavalcade of madness
forever your fate.

Departure

The glass is empty,
the song is sung,
the filter of my cigarette,
glows red with your
lipstick after burn.
The platform is deserted,
the train is pulling away,
no-one left
to wave goodbye
with silken scarf
nor breathy sigh,
or loving glance
nor kisses blown,
but left alone
forgotten and
prone.

Setting Sun

It troubles me,
this thought,
that you should suffer
and leave so soon.

It troubles me,
to pick up pen
stir emotions, write again,
as once I did
when passion and
conviction burned
loud and fierce.
I did not succumb,
I did not,
Yet, I just as surely did.

But this is about you
your pain, your suffering
to depart so soon
and be denied
the blessings that
conversation demands and avails
no protest.
Things to do as yet undone
'tis true and cruel this twist.

Embrace

The shards of my life,
sharp and glistening,
jagged edge and rapier,
pierce first through skin
then through bone.
They cut and scar me,
but bloodied, bruised and battered
I play their game.

This tortured anguish
in dark despair,
of deep desire,
in passion's lair,
so unfulfilled
but standing there,
a beauty of vision,
in auburn hair,
to beckon still
from beyond
the pale,
in shimmering white
with kindly stare.

The wanting,
the needing,
the hurting
it is deep.
To fill the night
and steal my sleep,
come a time when I will
join in perfect peace,
and rest divine
in your embrace.

Delicate

she weaves the stars
into her hair,
and moonlight
in her eyes.
with soft silken skin,
rose petal lips
and gentle hazel eyes,
she holds my time,
my tide
and my story
in her delicate hand.

Sleeping Muse

Thy princess stirs
in her robe of sleep.
Light feathers dust
wearily the drowsy away.
This gentle, delicate
rise and wane
each breath taken
slumber's release
of pain.

Siren

Hello,
my little boudoir babe
with kaleidoscope eyes
in crystal haze.
My seahorse dancing
black and green
summon the night in
shimmering sheen.
To glow and fold
in feathers pink
in silken flesh
we gently sink.

Celestial

She walks through fields of shadows
flickering in candlelight.
Far across the ballroom calling,
screams her love in passions flare.
High above the sky is calling
blinding flash of bright blue light.

Glowing in the night-time sky
a blanket of stars old and wise.
Beyond a haze of raindrop fears
tantalising for so many years,
grows the seed of love's sweet union
alone at last they freely dance.

Moonlit Shadowed Seas

Into the realm of darkness
flow moonlit shadowed seas.
Across a void of passion
her love sails from me.
No lighthouse beam
shines out to sea,
there's nothing left
here for me to be.
Accept the drowning,
the passion void
in moonlit
shallowed seas.

Enchanted

In the night
when the passion fuel's
all but spent
I reach to touch,
the angels sent
you.

The sweetest bond
of loving bliss,
surrendered to
the longing kiss.

Lying there in
blissful rest
I hear you call
for all that's left.

We feed the torch
the heaven's scent us
to hold, caress
and gently ease,
together.

And here we are
serene at peace
in dream-like land,
joyed by passion's release.

Euphoria

The thrill sends shivers
down my spine
blood and bone intertwine
lipstick lips and lovers' limbs
we join together.

Pearls

Strings of loves
on emotional chains
count the score
in this cruel game.
Alone.

Lovers meet
embrace, entangle
oblivious to their
lover's triangle
come.

Indiscretion
in the night
within the blackness
a blueing light
Outside.

Clutching straws
in love's bold dream
a vision of love
so seldom seen
here.

La Volta

In the darkness
when the line runs true
I think of love
I think of you.
I know your touch
your sensations spin
to feel the healing
let the love begin.

And in the saddest time
no despair,
your heart in mine
a time to heal,
and not to fear
come to touch,
an embrace so dear.

To hear the words
a kindness spoke
to share together
the loving gift
wash over us
like rain
to reign,
rebirth.

Serene Surrender

Sleep serenely,
forever breathing
in deepest slumber
I yearn for you.
For peace and love
none can give
tormented soul,
released to live.
So hold me deep
in floods
of space,
deep, surrender
and dark
waiting,
willingly
I return to
You.

If you enjoyed this nighttime sojourn
Take some time before the morn
Pray tell us what you felt this night
Please leave a review, before you take flight.

Index of Poems with First Lines

I
Welcome – You want dark, I can oblige. 2
Tempest – I am born of Fire and Tempest 3
Pendulum – I have heard of this (Happiness) 4
The Healing Despair – Feel the poison in the mist 5
Shhh – If it's dark it must be night 6
Blissful arrest – I feel a cold wind upon my back 7
Strange Days – The cavalcade of freaks 8
Divine Grotesque – Turn away, Now! 10
Phantom – What say you to this? 11
Ego eram – Something stirring in the gutter 12
Unfold – Making monsters in the corridors of our minds . . . 13
Vanquished – Hold fast you monsters! 14
Armchair Wrestling – Sitting in my armchair 16
acquiescence – Drawing blood and prickling pain 17
Alone – I walk the path alone 18
Invocation – Sometimes when I'm all alone 19
Silent Riposte – Say no more, I've heard it all before 21
Pigeon – Drowning is proportional 22
Endless – It is the time of darkness, a time of pain 23
Shadowlands – Walking through Shadowlands 24
Epitaph – These are not just words 25
Creation's darkness – Stars of darkness fill the night 26
Into The Black – On a distant planet, at the furthest shore . . . 27

II
Path less Travelled – The path which brought me here 30

Hypnotist – Haunting memories of the hypnotist 33
Vampire – Love me. Feed on me 34
The Haunting – It haunts me sometimes 35
Violin Concerto – The violin concerto screams 36
Poison – In a hollow empty room 37
Chasing Skies – Rendered fire and lightning 38
The Night Shades – Nothing's sacred outside the ivory tower . 39
Crows – "I was born before the crows 40
The Attic – Wind blows through broken attic windows 41
Redemption – How may I help you my Son 42
Dark, Heart, Ways (The Recital) – This cross I bear 44
Frosted Talons – Still, dark and still 46
Sacred sacraments – Sacred sallow Hallowed hours 47
Lost – Where once was love 49
Kraken – The Kraken rises, high from waters dark 50
Abbott Black – A little rhyme, a winter chill 51
Perpetual Endings -It is a dark night 52
Verité – Torment the dance in opiate haze 53
Silent Mirror – Green light shines in sodium haze 54
White Chipped Cup – In this cup of coffee 55
The Exquisite Devine – Hark, I hear an angel 56
Blessed Be – It is my craving. It is my need 57
My Evangeline – We touch and the darkness recoils 58
Tethered – Claustrophobic. That's how my brain feels. 59

III
The Unseen (or Beyond the Veil) – Walk with me, through fields
of glass 62
No Place Like Home – I love this place 63
Heroes – Emaciated heroes crave the limelight of the street . . 64
Glass Eyes – Walking down the side street show 65
The Actor – Black out sights from red lights grow 66

Fix – "How much for me?" the girl cried 68
Vesting – Pressure! Vice like 69
Beached – Sleazy dayglo of birds on the wing 70
Treadmill of Despair (A Butterfly Caught) – Siren scream, teenage SOS 72
Desolation Alley – Back on the streets ain't got no ties 74
Subway Rats – Lying in the subway with a switchblade 75
Strychnine Kids – Stalking the alleys like a Punch and
Judy show 76
Snowblind – See them all catch a fire 77
Streets – Streets that run with anger 78
Lazarus – Wispy shadows walk the boardwalk at night 79
Because We're Young – Because we're young 80
Trapped in Ecstasy – Martyred by your fashioned love 81
Stranger Danger – We talk of spies with shadowed eyes 82
Intricate – A Spider's Web of deceit and lies 83
Classifieds – Blood shot eyes, mourn lost decaying buildings . 84
Hope Eraser – A haze of light in the alley grows 85

IV

The Endless Beginnings – Open up the door and come inside . 88
Enchanting – Hidden in the darkness, by faintest candlelight . 89
Crimson – Red is the colour of my passion dream 90
Evermore – Hold the dream like a heart on fire 91
Amore – Between the sheets behind closed curtains 92
Red Rose – How sweet the perfume graces me 93
Deserts – A cloak of darkness hides the tears 94
Prayer – "He lies in bed never looking at me 95
Medusa – In the world of darkness 96
Blissful Cataclysm – What pain is this that taunts me now? . . 97
Carousel – She moves just like 98
Breathe – "Breathe in, breathe in the dark 99

Cat O' Nine Tails – Lipstick words upon the mirror 101
Crush – Belts and buckles and 102
Frenzy – A feeding frenzy 103
Killing Zone – In the killing zone 104
Black is the ardour – Black is the ardour cold as ice 105
Departure – The glass is empty, the song is sung 106
Setting Sun – It troubles me, this thought 107
Embrace – The shards of my life, sharp and glistening 108
Delicate – she weaves the stars into her hair 110
Sleeping Muse – Thy princess stirs in her robe of sleep 111
Siren – Hello, my little boudoir babe 112
Celestial – She walks through fields of shadows 113
Moonlit Shadowed Seas – Into the realm of darkness 114
Enchanted – In the night when the passion fuel's 115
Euphoria – The thrill sends shivers 116
Pearls – Strings of loves on emotional chains 117
La Volta – In the darkness when the line runs true 118
Serene Surrender – Sleep serenely, forever breathing 119

About the Author

Derek R. King is a multi-genre, award-winning poet and author, as well as a photographer and a musician. He lives in Scotland with his wife, Julie L. Kusma, where they enjoy the great outdoors, long walks in the hills, going to seaside, art, and taking pictures for some of their books.

Poetry Collections
Soulmates Forevermore (Love Poetry)
New Year's Frost (Seasonal Poetry)
Forevermore (Love Poetry)
In Sun & Shade (Nature Poetry
More Red Roses (Love Poetry)
Urban (City-Nature Poetry)
The Elegy (Dark Poetry)
Twelve Red Roses in Verse (Love Poetry)
Natyre Boy (Nature Poetry)
Noir [Or, When the Night Comes] (Gothic Poetry)

Nonfiction
The Life and Times of Clyde Kennard
(Biographical-American Civil Rights)

Follow this Author

http://DerekRKing.uk
https://x.com/DerekRKing2
https://www.instagram.com/derekrking2/

DEREK R KING
POET | AUTHOR

If you enjoyed this book, you might like…

Collaborations

Educational
(K)no(w)where: Manifestation Made Easy
Our Dinosaurs: Discoveries, Distinctions, & More
Our Planets: Moons, Myths, & More
Our Trees: Botanics, Beliefs, & More

Poetry
Autumn's Splendor
Love on A Winter's Night
LOVE is LOVE

Keepsakes
Our Spring: Imagination, Creativity, & More
Our Summer: Adventures, Amusements, & More
Our Halloween: Mysteries, Monster, & More
Our Christmas: Traditions, Memories, & More

Inspirational
The Rings We Carry: Poetic Reflections of Growth & Resilience
Bloom: Ho'oponopono Words of Love & Gratitude
Life is Sweet: Words of Gratitude
Slag and Other Worthy Things
Ho'oponopono: Words to Forgive & Love
Kintsugi: Healing Affirmations for Our World
Even Only Besides
Tranquil Seas: Still Yourself and Be
Nectar: Words of Self-Love and Care
Moonrise to Moonset and All the Stars in Between
Sunrise to Sunset and All the Hours in Between
Holoi 'ikepili Words to Release and Cleanse
Buddha's Garden: Allowing & Non-Attachment Haiku
with love, the Universe
Honey: Words to Heal & Mend

The Lighter Half Series
Angel Prayers, Volume 5
Illusion, Volume 4
Alpha, Volume 3
More Amore, Volume 2.1
Amore, Volume 2
Abracadabra, Volume 1

www.ingramcontent.com/pod-product-compliance
Lightning Source LLC
Chambersburg PA
CBHW032038040426
42449CB00007B/934